Lantern Lit series
Vol. 1

Dog On A Chain Press

James H. Duncan
Mat Gould
John Dorsey

Printed in the United States of America

First printing 2014

ISBN 978-0-9855291-4-7

Dog On A Chain Press
c/o Beasley Barrenton
503 Silverleaf Rd.
Zionville, NC 28698

For ordering information (Publisher Direct) or all other inquiry
dogonachainpress@yahoo.com
http://dogonachainpress.tumblr.com

for contributor credits/permission see back page(s)

"this life is slow…wake the fuck up and have a breath, prepare to makeshift"

-Bazzel Bumgarden

The Darkest Bomb

Poems
by
James H. Duncan

Seasick on 46th

...and then crossing Fifth Avenue as
big dollop raindrops hit the pavement like
face slaps falling from a seasick green
sky casting a surreal dim over the streets
and alleys in Manhattan, and there is
a thickening of air as if the walls are
closing in—the halal cart vendors stamp
their feet and turn their eyes skyward, steam
rising from their grills—the ice cream vendor
pulls her frostie truck away from the curb
and drives away down 46th street, as if there
is any escape in any direction for anyone
—stepping inside a café with a second-floor
seating area, where men spilled from their
seats from too much paper bag booze and
businesswomen wound up tight gossip
about the traps and tantrum teakettles teasing
them at home and there is a cute ponytailed woman reading a book
and she looks up for just one moment revealing
her cold water Atlantic heartbeat dense with
razors and dreams leftover from little
girl heartaches and letdowns, which give
off all kinds of warning signs, and the rain
begs against the windows for our love and affection,
but no one pays any notice, they just drink and talk
and melt into newspapers full of empty columns
that say nothing about the water running down
the streets and into the gutters and someday
back into the sky where the dollop raindrops
will fall bleak on the remains of the Berlin
Wall, will fall sorrowful on Congo refugees, will
fall incensed on the back of a breaching killer whale
off the Antarctic coast, and Fifth Avenue might still be
around then, might not, although if it isn't, wondering
why the rain begs so hard against the windows of
the world will be the least of our human worries

Marksman and the Moth

a dead moth clings to the wall and
I begin reading through old journals,
lick my thumb,
engage the delusory pages
and turn on all the trembling filaments
of the past, alighting old fears
and seeing a liar, a seeker,
a marksman, a piper,
finding judgments and scathing desires,
moments alive no more and maybe
never were,
each inkblot a fired shot
each page a dead thing
come back to life to whisper
what could have been
what never will

I close the journal and
snap off the lamp to stare into
the middle distance

as moths tremble
in the darkness all around
me

So rare, an empty sky

the women have a way
of appearing in the mind
months, years later
often when a word in
a newspaper, a city name
perhaps, comes up
then you will remember
what Minnesota winters
felt like before you
aborted in the final moment
walked back to your car
and turned south

or how it felt drinking
beer along a river
on the front range
of Colorado, also
in the wintertime,
to feel the grip of green
glass and the back
of her head, pulling
her lips closer

or how the pavement rapped
hollow underfoot in
Cambridge at night, long
after the trains stopped,
long after the lights
went out, and then the
creaking of the stairs
to an empty room
in a full bed and breakfast
the absence of her
stronger than her presence
ever *ever* was

or the sound of the heater
clicking patiently

as she sleeps, as you sit
and listen to the rain
simmer against the window
a blood-red maple leaf
embracing the rippled pane
blocking out the moon's
specter upon the lake
across the cow field
down the road,
as she sleeps, as you
sit, both dreaming
of what could have been

something as simple as a city
name or even the color
of a woman's shirt,
the memories ignite behind
the eyes, shapeless
eternal clouds;
one minute there, the next
they wisp away, circling
around the globe until
a name overheard, or just
the way the newest adoration
wears her mousy brown hair,
brings them across the
horizon once again
untouchable and opaque

Dishwater for the vase

there you are in the bottom of the glass
your final stare smooth as melting ice
the barkeep is plunging tumblers
into the gray dishwater, filthy gray as he,
filthy gray as his lungs, plunging toxin
sharp into the meat of the heart

somewhere a broken dog I knew is sleeping
his tail snapped in the wind of human blackness
his dreams take place in a field where
he will never run free
this weighs upon both of us, forever

Frank Sinatra sings
Frank Sinatra is dead
Frank Sinatra is laughing in the men's room
at what he wrote on the wall

and there you are, looking up from the glass
cringing at the immoderate stench of smoke ballasting the air
you always were more sunflower than rose
more lily in a vase than cattail in the mire

Willie Nelson sings, Willie Nelson is not dead
but he will be one day
and you
and so will I, and in that grave
will be one empty box
along with plenty of dirt
to keep this empty glass company
but I won't know for sure

up from the ice and the smoke, you rise
and as I stand to follow you out the door
change falls to the floor from a hole
in the right coat pocket
the barkeep looks up from his sink
no one is there

Cockroaches and I

where
  in the hell do these
cockroaches
  come from?

they appear
  out
of nowhere
    on the floor
as if forsaken by
some
      sneering god
from above,
        left to die
  in my kitchen

where are
  all the paper towels
and newspapers
when I need them?
  they always hang
around in piles before
    the phantasmal visitations
come for me,
    never after

the light bulbs
    burn out
left and
  right here,
and while I'd rather be
  blind
than
  see these things,
feeling
    them
against my
  feet

would be worse

and why do they choose
    to die here?
then again,
        here I am
                dying
            every day and night,
and for what?
    to pick up the rice-paper
    cockroaches
every day and night?

in death,
    I wonder,
who
    will pick me up
when I burn
    out the final
bulb
    and leave my
        husk
in the dark?

who?
    you?
or maybe we
        will die together,
    the cockroaches and I,
if we are
    lucky,
maybe,
    but who gets
lucky
    these days?

The darkest bomb of all

it claws; the sharp foolishness of falling
into idiot dreams of being a soldier,
dreams of broken highways and
women weeping streams of sunlight
and flowers and standing on hills looking down
at the eviscerated soldiers, courage wasted, my own
corpse rising, limping off toward the border where
consciousness waits; a white-flag dawn

and the next day, another kind of battle,
another kind of death march through
another kind of country torn with weariness
and endless, endless suffering, crosses,
flags, sponsors, checks in the mail

never understanding
never witnessing the end of the battle
never reaching the other shore
a shore that does not exist
just the eyes closing and rolling into
the back of the head
the windows sliding shut
whispers from the staircase
claws sinking in
the darkest bomb of all

Theft

the dead release their names to me
sing praise to the sun of tomorrow
no bite and no quarrel resound as they share
the full, the middle, the last

these things we don't hear, the unbound
local vocabulary of a graying modern age

the higher the branch, the further we roam
into time, space, and colloquialism

Otis Jefferson Portsmouthe
Phillip Maynard Toth
Patricia Olin Odsman
Aaron Anternoch

on brittle page or roughcast in stone
an offer unrequited
an acceptance long-awaited
in the north, with frigid hands
and the south, heated wishes
small offerings from holiday idols
worshipped with full skulls
festive smoke and hollowed fears
Mexican holy rites and confetti

I'll use you, I'll use you all
your name is not forgotten, only
reused and pardoned
given new limbs, second chances
in the pages, in the minds

someone will inevitably sing
your song tonight
every night
the notes held aloft and hailed as
saviors of the living and the dead

Rumination

the nights when it rains feel better
as if the earth has bled a little, too

leaves bobbing with teary weight
and the cats skitter damply
avoiding brush, light, Man alike

the moon alone is dry
drifting over mourning, somnolent homes
empty rooms wondering why the wounds
came so sudden
so silent, now soothed
cleansed by the midnight moon's yawning gaze

The Incident at Choke Cherry Farm

death and distance are such
vital cogs these days

with a cold command
the dawn rises on sleepless
aimless raw red eyes

fingers stop the hands of the watch
water runs dry from the well
sulfur fumes coil from lit matches

death and distance howl hymns
across the prairie, and the gears
spin the sun away, the moon above,
the hatchet down, the echo out

and the wind carries black butterflies
of tinder and skin beyond the fence posts
such vital cogs these days,
such vital days, alas

Cemetery Row

how many old men can you wake up on the couch
only to bury the next day beneath an armada of white dandelions
as jackrabbit thunderstorms rage within our hearts and
our father's fathers listen through the toppled stones

lucky enough if only one, and even that one-pronged
pitchfork screams submission years before the bite, raw
nerve damage at the breakfast table in June, or gathering
wood in November snowstorms, thinking about nightmares
where caskets spoke to no one but you, you alone carrying
the burden of a one-sided conversation with raw clay and dust

but what of the others? what of the voices from the hall?
the long cemetery procession of leather mitts and wrenches,
men of generations past who took you in and fed you, gave
you second chances, money, steel in your bones, memories
of winters in the woods with a gun in your hands, icy verve;
how many feet of dirt separate the men from all the boys?

while some leapt from Hudson bridges, others stuck around
and sat on front lawns and counted dandelion heads popping in
the breeze until the night came, closing summer pools forever,
on and on, the fathers call, fathers drive, fathers man the grill
but those ballgame Halloween memories come with a price

for what comes for one will come for all,
a procession of men descending into dirt
white dandelions on the wind

One day my broken neck will come for me

what your husband didn't know
certainly hurt like hell when his fist
found the hollow of my face

I felt I deserved it before it even hit home
the hammer of knuckles and force cathartic,
the sting an easy pleasure after
all of that whiskey and the tangle
of your legs, your panting against my neck

intoxicated, I let him swing a few more times,
and I didn't laugh because I knew he was
in hell now, burning with sorrow and hate

I'd been there before, felt that same betrayal
and I think that's why I let him have his due
because I never got mine, and because I should
have known so much better, and when he
turned his fury on you I picked up my bundled
clothes and slipped out the door, walking

naked to my car in the neighbor's driveway;
the air felt good, the cold wash flowing down
from a full blue-ice moon like a slumbering
giant's surprised eye at the sound of a skirting
mouse in his play-world trying to sneak away

maybe that's why the husband appeared behind me
with a knife—he'd obtained an immortal tip-off
so I jumped in my car, reversed through the white
picket fence at top speed, and drove home in a drunken
fog of self-loathing and your delicate lilac perfume

West of Waco, twenty miles

pass the hermit tumbleweeds and park the car
cross the fence-line barricade of rusted
and spiked twine, thin as floss in the blue winter
wind, screaming a swallowed name across
the prairie, razor wire limping through the dust

and maybe there are other cars somewhere 'round
there, and they might make noises, doors and humans
groping forward toward death, but forget those
jack-in-the-box melodies, they're nothing to the sound
of the names floating through the wires, through
the stunted pine trees squatting in the yellow dirt
stubble on the drunken wino earth walking home on
Wednesday from a Friday paycheck, money burned,
lighting a cigarette from the sun, the ashes falling,
chasseing across the highway toward that ramshackle
home built of driftwood in the desert heartland heartbeat
heart residing between dusty lung lamentations

keep walking, and when you find yourself beyond all that ash and
human noise, deciding between the car waiting by the silver thread
highway leading south or the prairie forever
…just keep on walking into that wide expanse of grateful nothing, not
caring to open your eyes to see the state border
ripping open a failed suture, and know it'll sew itself
back up a dry-blood beauty of a scar when you wake
up on the other side of that solitary existence

Dry Tide

great dead whales full of bones
lie praying with the sun breaking in
through briny teeth

the holy fisherman cannot hook us all

some seek to rot in the belly
rather than fry in the pan
and the cool waters are long ago gone
the tide in remembrance, hurts
knee deep, waves clasped

those great dead whales full of bones
decaying with the sunlight in their guts

James H Duncan is the founding editor of *Hobo Camp Review: Poetry & Prose from the Road.* When not wandering late-night cafes, corner pubs, and train station platforms, James is an editor for *Writer's Digest* as well as a novelist and a short story writer, and in 2013 he released his debut collection of short fiction, *The Cards We Keep.* He is a Pushcart and Best of the Net nominee and has published his work in such magazines as *Apt, The Battered Suitcase, The Gap-Toothed Madness, Haggard & Halloo, Plainsongs, Red Fez, San Pedro River Review, Zygote in My Coffee, Thick With Conviction,* and *Underground Voices,* among others. This is his seventh collection of poetry. More of his poetry, books, and information about his upcoming novels may be found at jameshduncan.blogspot.com.

Sermon from a Thundering Brim

Poems
by
Mat Gould

the universe itself laments

the day goes down as it does
full of sun
full of clouds
full of gray underneath everything
full of holding onto what there is to keep
full of sleep and waking up to what there is to see
what there is to feel
what there is to know
what there is to forget

all of these things in a bunch
burning in barrels
burning along the roadside
burning across the landscape
smoke emanating from massive stone canon towers

yet this is not the entire sky
not the entire day
but the sky is full
full of whatever else there is
a gallery of pastel prints-

the following of tanks

I have not asked the riot to ease up
nor disperse
should it not be allowed to do as it will?
most of us, being people, do the same
either in supposed seclusion
or gaggling uproariously in a parade of self-assured existence

seek
this
verse
through the (p)ages

apes punching at the ground
soldiers surrounding the synagogue
hokey pokey
and
ring around the rosy
the world ends all too often these days-

clarity defines half of the days fate

a face in the sun is charmed
even as the wind
scrapes cold teeth against these bones

no need to cross any rivers today
no need to see the mountains
from any closer than out off into the prevalent distance
no need to replenish the cupboards that are nearing empty

if there is not enough marrow
too feed the cat
the fat will be bled-

one does not need all of his teeth to stay on his feet

old again
something feels funny
youth putting up a fight
'filling the hole with punches'

dirt tastes like dirt
as much as a bad taste in the mouth is because
of the dirt eaten
willingly

and not spit out
taken to oath, the good ole iron gut-

sparring with the 'and then some'

8:30 in broad daylight
I take a piss off the porch
the hostas are thriving
a mist has crept into the early evening
cooling off the hillsides

I have a few thoughts
other than the blatant facts of the aforementioned
I figure on keeping them mostly to myself-

rubble bubble

buried under
tossing stones
large rocks though not quite boulders

what else would I be doing
standing atop
doing my best King Kong
fighting Godzilla to a draw

these are not styrofoam concrete
no
these are upon shoulders, back collapsing
entrenched in the ground up until the avalanche
let
go

and to think, all of this from wet dust-

symbol of a fortune is a coin in the drain

secrets pertaining to this remain between the gutter
and the rain
let no blood dry

the jester is at rest
stacking the fire
and hiding in the smoke
pulling his ghost closer to the chest

it is not the blanket that keeps us warm
but
readily
enough
death
keeps us alive

under the sun
the horizon deepens-

over the counter

five packets of sugar
one drop of cream
and a warm up in the mug
I had to give that black shit up
along with most of the other shit
that kept me at the diner all night in the first place
a decision I doan generally reconsider

but lately it's a vagary none the less

two eggs
over easy
with hot sauce
butter and apple jelly on the toast

so,
this plate in front of me
is gonna have to do
I haven't any more room for hunger-

no signs for heaven

caterpillar in the pickle jar
you will become a butterfly before I do
I will open the lid
let you fly amongst the starving void

watch out for the weasel
the fisherman
the owl
they will want to eat you
or use as fodder for

the art of stumbling abound through Samsara
is
not to be made meal of
because of your beauty or your fattened hind-

chasing air

cheating the over under is jes taking a guess

choke out the fire
by
beating it with a rug
whatever may be still fusillades in flames.

admirable how the blaze keeps up with the high haunched hare
all the way until the sea
where heat meets salt
ash and sand compromise-

a beacon of life

mouths drinking from hands cupped

taking care of what there is to take care of
a deed that must be done
a work that is never finished

the bending of faith

it takes two hands to move these stones
and even then
one will need a spine that is prepared for both plow and
redemption

the seed need be anchored into this crude ground
furrowed deep enough
to reap from the grist of heels digging in-

fighting over the worm

sitting by the door, filling the room with what else but the sun
this is it
a great American poem

pure
sure with intent
hair yet to be messed
seconds before the scrum

trying to figure on a means to get the handle, where to start to try
and win the trite damn war
polishing the trigger
packing the muzzle
an ear to the ground
a bloodshot eye on the ridge

all but the far off is quiet
the For'd, Harch is over
now, for the splurging banter of men divining mortar
their dying words discordant

sitting by the door, filling the room with what else but the sun
the chair scuttling as I get up to check the kettle
I prefer to catch it before it whistles-

cold pizza in my teeth

I just want to see words

daylight no longer at ease
change occurs, doesn't last long
thank you bird outside my dormant window for rattling your little
body with hormonal glee

cartwheels are still hard for me to do
I don't know if it is heavy shoes
or lack of shoulder mobility
half way over I slump and crumble

life will be simpler
I can find it within myself to pass it off as such
a primordial moment agasp

until then
remain weary
fight the shadows
growl with a wet mouth
come up lame, walk it off
curse with sentiment
laugh with senility
break into fever,
add the sweat to what is left of the burning lamp oil

snarl and itch
yes, snarl and itch-

mumbling these types of things out loud and trying to make it home before I am dead

the marching band sends off the trumpets
brings on the twirling rifles
stops to shoot
salute
to standing guard

needing to get through this day half alive by the end of it
consecrates the revelation that myths do not exist

the marching band sends off the trumpets
brings in the riot gear
halts
stands in front of me vying to get to the store
for bread-

afternoon coffee

this could really change the day
but not the dirty face of the building
and not the dying branches of the wintering trees

warmth in the bones
and meat underneath the skin
may very well keep me from sinking
into the colds bitter hint
its salted dry draft
against my grit

a taste of blood
a daydreams revival
one sip in-

the bombs are complimentary

who laid iron to sink
buried under the loyal sod
box cars left at the end of the line
a ghost town of no ghosts
there is no way now to come back

high grass bending over with heavy seed
and thistle
every child is old born to this land
youth is bold
entranced by electric concrete pyramids

never looking up
for overhead there is an oceanic black-hole
dark skies
in the eyes of watery eyed beauts

shrapnel is of no surprise
the fireworks disperse a scarce luminance upon the outskirts
an outline of a familiar face flashes against a barren dawn

it is safe now to cross the street
and make it back inside the bunker-

pretty is as pretty is

soft light drifting
out
the night returns

the gift
this pulse
is a tender interlude

lanterns
above
the sea
out
of reach

never could we
imagine
falling as fast-

Mat Gould is currently hunkered in on a gravel road up the other side of a mountain, feeding the hyena and whittling poems into a sharp point. He keeps a close eye on his own with a steady yet at times drunken aim. He has authored 4 books of poetry exclusively for Dog On A Chain Press.

Books by **Mat Gould/Dog On A Chain Press**:

Lantern In The Half Night Sky
It Will Be The Lion
The Fire is Breathing On Me
A Blackbird Sings the Blues With Laughter

...and a yet to be scheduled for release complete text:
Sucking On The Fat of Life (escorting the immortal toward the door) that compiles his first D.O.A.C.P release (currently unavailable) with works written within and during his four titles up to and including "Sermon..."

He can be contacted via Dog On A Chain Press.

HAPPY HOUR
MADRIGALS

POEMS
BY
JOHN DORSEY

Drunk John

gave me $7 and a cigar snip
for my 25th birthday
the morning his girlfriend
kicked him out
of their spruce street apartment.

the year before
i'd watched as she passed him
love notes in hindi
across the bar
while he listened
to iggy pop
on the jukebox
as it rained outside.

i could swear he was crying
when he sang happy birthday
under the busted street light.

Sarah

had meth teeth
& an ass that hadn't quit
since just after vietnam.

she had barely finished the 10th grade
and was as good a therapist
as anyone with an ivy league degree
and she could pour a drink

like the virgin mary.

Creepy Steve

looked like an albino
on heroin.

he would start the day
with a boilermaker
before launching into stories
about how the government
was paying outer space aliens
to abduct nazi war criminals.

half way through he'd fall asleep.

he told me that if i ever needed
a job in argentina
to just let him know.

Bill

had spent the best months of his life
in the hanoi hotel

he would start crying
as he signed over his check
to the bar

imagining bombs dropping
from the sky.

twisting off the cap
on his beer bottle

now, that was fireworks.

Oscar

had a house in mexico
and would invite me
to run dope every year
as a summer job.

he'd say, "it builds character, you'll
know what you're made of."

in the end
i was a coward.

Mary Ellen

wore an eye patch
and hung paintings on the wall
just above my barstool.

she noticed the little things
like the moon hung crooked
on your lips

and all of the little ghosts
in our eyes.

Clark

was a famous newspaper columnist
i watched him take college kids
for beer money
as jazz filled the air

i learned more about ethics
by watching him sink an 8 ball
than i ever did
in the classroom.

Dana

smelled like hippie sweat
the night we made out
listening to jimmy bruno
after she bought me
my first guinness.

a few days later
she was busted
with pot in her dorm room
& was gone forever

but i still have jazz
in my heart.

Alex

had worked at the bar
since he was in high school

at his own wedding
he stopped dancing
with his wife
to pour everyone a drink

old habits die hard.

Tommy

i took ken in for pitcher of beer
before putting him on the greyhound.

thirty minutes later
everyone was held at gunpoint
i watched Tommy from behind the bar
refusing to give up his wallet
even with a 9mm riding shotgun
against his temple.

after the robbers had gone
he went outside to stand in the sun.

he said, "it's beautiful out there."
and then came back in
and bought everyone
a drink

it was beautiful.

Ed

once asked me to read poetry in the bar
i told him "I don't spill blood in cathedrals, unless
somebody is willing to clean it up."

he turned away laughing
slipped a quarter
in the jukebox
and never asked again.

Fred

wrote freedom songs
marched on washington
for civil rights.

now he could barely
walk a straight line
after 2pm.

Jessica

taught french poetry
to the bridge and tunnel crowd
sipped warm beer
& fingered herself to bukowski
in the bathroom

she said
she got moist
at the sight of a tool belt

the only blue collar
thing about her

was her credit score.

Marc

had worked for nasa
now his orbit
spanned the entire length
of the bar.

he'd get drunk on highballs
& pabst blue ribbon
until he saw stars
everywhere

Gary

christina and i watched gary
sing ac/dc covers
the first time we held hands.

she sat sipping a corona
& i told her
that i wasn't drinking anymore
that when i looked into her eyes

i felt drunk
without having to run up a tab
that ours was a love

done dirt cheap.

Harold

could've had any woman
in the bar

instead he just kept drinking
waiting for a happy hour
that never came.

John Dorsey is the author of several collections of poetry, including "Teaching the Dead to Sing: The Outlaw's Prayer" (Rose of Sharon Press, 2006), "Sodomy is a City in New Jersey" (American Mettle Books, 2010), "Leaves of Ass" (Unadorned Press, 2011) and, most recently, "Tombstone Factory" (Epic Rites Press, 2013). His work has been nominated for the Pushcart Prize. He may be reached at archerevans@yahoo.com

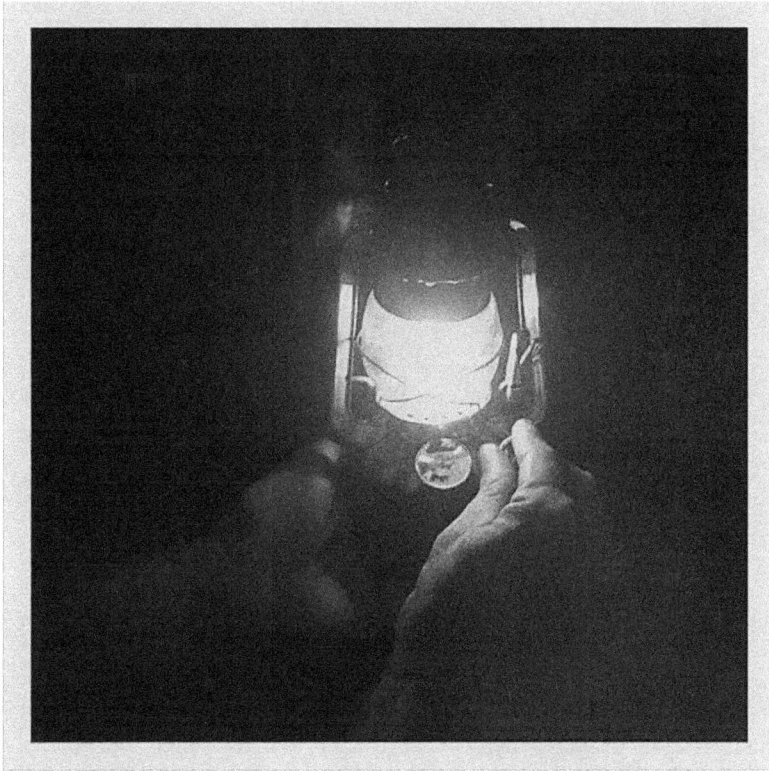

Photo: Abby White-Gould
Cover: layout: Ryan Bradley, design: Beasley Barrenton
Cover Art: Simon Prades: Graphic Design/Artist born in 1985 into a German/Spanish family, is a freelance illustrator for clients in Editorial, Advertising and Film while teaching drawing and illustration at the university of applied sciences in Trier, Germany.

The manuscripts for this -Lantern Lit series- have been personally sought, hunted for their pelt, and selected by me from poets I am genuinely enthralled to work with, poets that are poets at the basis and gnarl of their being, Poets who cannot help but be such, poets that will continue singing the gospel of real life shit, poets commanding the ship from wherever it is that they may deliberate, roaring out to a bird on the wire as if that bird is everyman at the pier of their own existence.

Keep a lantern lit,
Beasley Barrenton

www.ingramcontent.com/pod-product-compliance
Lightning Source LLC
Chambersburg PA
CBHW020522030426
42337CB00011B/507